CORNERSTONES OF FREEDOM™

D0568607

GETTYSBURG

BY JOSH GREGORY

CHILDREN'S PRESS®
An Imprint of Scholastic Inc.
New York   Toronto   London   Auckland   Sydney
Mexico City   New Delhi   Hong Kong
Danbury, Connecticut

Content Consultant
James Marten, PhD
Professor and Chair, History Department
Marquette University
Milwaukee, Wisconsin

Library of Congress Cataloging-in-Publication Data

Gregory, Josh.
  Gettysburg/by Josh Gregory.
     p. cm.—(Cornerstones of freedom)
  Includes bibliographical references and index.
  ISBN-13: 978-0-531-25034-1 (lib. bdg.)   ISBN-10: 0-531-25034-2 (lib. bdg.)
  ISBN-13: 978-0-531-26559-8 (pbk.)   ISBN-10: 0-531-26559-5 (pbk.)
  1. Gettysburg, Battle of, Gettysburg, Pa., 1863—Juvenile literature.
. Title.
  E475.53.G74 2012
  973.7'349—dc22   2011010751

  2 3 4 5 6 7 8 9 10 R 21 20 19 18 17 16 15 14 13 12

Photographs © 2012: Alamy Images: 44 (Nancy Hoyt Belcher), 49 (Ivy
Close Images), 40 (Niday Picture Library), 54, 59 (North Wind Picture
Archives), 35 (H.A. Ogden/Classic Image); AP Images: 51 (Carolyn
Kaster), 12, 28, 58 (North Wind Picture Archives); Bridgeman Art Library
International Ltd., London/New York: 4 top, 41 (Timothy O'Sullivan/© British
Library Board. All Rights Reserved), 5 top, 27 (Private Collection/© Civil
War Archive); Getty Images: 2, 3, 36 (Buyenlarge), 15 (Kean Collection),
50 (Fletcher C. Ransom/Library of Congress), 8 (Stock Montage); Josh
Gregory: 64; Library of Congress: 43 (George N. Barnard), 5 bottom, 30, 57
Brady National Photographic Art Gallery, Washington D.C.), 46 (Alonzo
Chappel), 11 (Currier & Ives), 17 (Henszey & Co.), 32 (H.A. Ogden/F.E.
Wright), 24, 38 (Timothy O'Sullivan), 42 (William Morris Smith), 23 (Alfred R.
Vaud), 20, 29; Media Bakery: 18 (C. Borland/PhotoLink), back cover (Greg
Dale), 19; North Wind Picture Archives: 7 (William L. Sheppard), 25, 56;
PictureHistory.com: 47; Richard T. Nowitz: cover; The Granger Collection,
New York: 4 bottom, 34 (L. Valdemar Fischer), 26 (Edwin Forbes), 22 (Kurz
& Allison), 16 (ullstein bild), 6, 10, 37, 48; The Image Works/Mary Evans

Did you know that studying history can be fun?

BRING HISTORY TO LIFE by becoming a history investigator. Examine the evidence (primary and secondary source materials); cross-examine the people and witnesses. Take a look at what was happening at the time—but be careful! What happened years ago might suddenly become incredibly interesting and change the way you think!

Contents

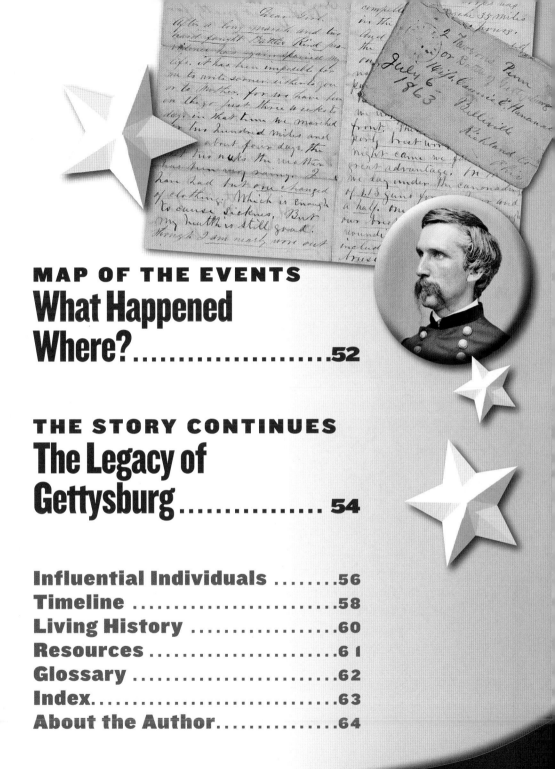

A Divided Nation

After the Revolutionary War, the states were united under a federal government.

In 1776, the 13 English colonies in North America declared themselves independent from Great Britain. Each colony became an independent state upon achieving victory in the American Revolutionary War (1775–1783). The states formed a single nation called the United States of America. They also shared a central government. But each state created its own laws based on the desires of its people. As years passed, social, political, and economic differences between the states began to cause divisions within the country. The

SLAVES WERE FIRST BROUGHT

U.S. government also acquired new territories. New states were added to the Union.

The growing number of differences between the states began to have a strong impact on American society. The practice of slavery became a critical issue. A fairly large majority of the states did not allow slavery. But a large percentage of newly occupied U.S. territories did. Slavery was essential to the economy in southern states.

The divisions within the country over issues such as slavery would drive the nation into a bloody **civil war**.

By the 19th century, slavery had become a controversial issue across the country.

CHAPTER 1

HIGH STAKES

Many people encouraged their state governments to secede from the Union.

NUMEROUS ATTEMPTS HAD BEEN made by the mid-19th century to reach a **compromise** between slave and non-slave states and territories. Many people on both sides of the issue believed slave states and free states could not exist in the same country. The debate grew more and more heated. Many people from the North, where slavery was not allowed, argued to simply outlaw slavery. Many Southerners suggested that their states secede, or leave, the Union. They hoped to form their own nation in which slavery would be legal.

Abraham Lincoln and Stephen Douglas tackled the slavery issue head-on in their debates.

A New President

The slavery debate was a key issue in the political campaigns of the time. Abraham Lincoln campaigned against Stephen Douglas in 1858 for a U.S. Senate seat in Illinois. The two candidates debated the issue of slavery. "A house divided against itself cannot stand," Lincoln said. "I believe the government cannot endure permanently half slave and half free."

Lincoln lost the 1858 election, but he became well recognized as a national political figure. He was elected president of the United States in 1860. One of his most important goals was to prevent the country from breaking apart. But several Southern states seceded from the Union before Lincoln took office in March 1861. These states believed Lincoln's election spelled the end of slavery and the destruction of the Southern economy.

On December 20, 1860, South Carolina became the first state to secede. Mississippi, Florida, Alabama, Georgia, Louisiana, and Texas also seceded by February 1, 1861. Representatives from the states met on February 4 to create a new government. They called it the Confederate States of America. Former

Abraham Lincoln and Stephen Douglas debated each other in seven different locations throughout Illinois during the 1858 Senate campaign. Each debate lasted about three hours. Douglas believed that states and territories should decide for themselves whether or not to allow slavery.

Douglas also claimed that Lincoln's ideas were too extreme and would only make the division within the country worse. Lincoln lost the election that year. But the debates became an important part of his successful presidential campaign two years later.

U.S. senator and U.S. secretary of war Jefferson Davis was appointed its president.

Upon taking office, Lincoln refused to admit that the seceded Confederate states were no longer part of the United States. "No state, upon its own mere motion, can lawfully get out of the Union," he said.

Civil War

A handful of Union-controlled military bases still existed in the South. One of these was Fort Sumter in South Carolina. Soon after taking office, Lincoln was asked by

The Union troops tried to hold Fort Sumter, but were eventually forced to surrender.

the fort's commander to send needed supplies. Lincoln had two options. He could supply the fort but risk an attack by Confederate military forces. He could also withdraw the fort's troops into Union territory. Lincoln ordered that Fort Sumter be resupplied.

Confederate forces attacked Fort Sumter on April 12, 1861. The American Civil War had officially begun. Virginia, Arkansas, Tennessee, and North Carolina immediately seceded and joined the Confederacy. The remaining 23 Union states prepared to forcefully retake the 11 Confederate states. Lincoln called for volunteer soldiers to join the fight. Seventy-five thousand additional men soon **enlisted** in the Union army.

The United States and the Confederate States of America battled one another for the next two years. Neither side gained a clear advantage. The Confederates' strategy was to defend their states against Union

A FIRSTHAND LOOK AT
A FORT SUMTER POLITICAL CARTOON

Representatives from the newly seceded state of South Carolina met with President James Buchanan in December 1860. Buchanan was going to leave office when Lincoln became president the next March. In this political cartoon, South Carolina governor Francis Pickens threatens Buchanan by saying, "Mr. President, if you don't surrender that fort at once, I'll be blowed if I don't fire." Buchanan responds, "Oh don't! Governor Pickens, don't fire! till I get out of office." See page 60 for a link to view the original cartoon.

A VIEW FROM ABROAD

Great Britain came close to joining the side of the Confederacy during the Civil War. The British had a strong trade relationship with the Southern states. They purchased large amounts of tobacco and cotton from Southern growers. Confederate diplomats worked to convince both Great Britain and France to support them in the war.

In 1861, two Confederate diplomats were taken from a British ship by U.S. naval forces. This almost caused Britain to join the war on the side of the South. U.S. diplomat Charles F. Adams was able to persuade them to stay **neutral**. No foreign nation joined either side during the Civil War.

takeover. They did not work to seize new territory. They simply wished to make the United States recognize their secession and leave them to their own government. The Union believed that the seceded states would be forced to rejoin the Union if it could gain control of major Southern cities.

Robert E. Lee

Confederate general Robert E. Lee commanded the Army of Northern Virginia. Lee's army operated mainly in Virginia. It was one of the most successful branches of the Confederate military. He developed a plan in the summer of 1863 to attack Union territory. It would be the first time during the war that a battle was fought on free soil. Lee believed that winning a major battle in the North would break the Union army's fighting spirit.

Charles F. Adams played a major role in diplomacy between the Union and Great Britain during the war.

Lee also had an eye toward the events that were currently unfolding to the west. After two years of fighting, Union forces were starting to make a significant gain into Southern territory along the Mississippi River. Lee knew that western Union forces would have to pull back and help defend against his attacks if he became a threat to the Union along the East Coast. Lee began moving his army of 75,000 men northward out of the Shenandoah Valley area of Virginia in June 1863. They engaged in several battles with Union troops and raided towns for supplies as they made their way toward Pennsylvania.

George G. Meade

Lee knew that his forces would eventually come into contact with Union general Joseph Hooker's Army of the Potomac. Lee had defeated Hooker about a month earlier at the Battle of Chancellorsville, in Virginia. He had less than half the number of men that Hooker had. Even so, Lee was confident that he would be victorious once again.

General Lee (front row, with white hair and beard) was one of the Confederacy's most successful military leaders.

But Lincoln removed Hooker from command of the Army of the Potomac on June 28. General George G. Meade was appointed to take his place. Lincoln had been unhappy with Hooker's losses. He hoped that Meade would be a more effective leader.

Lee's troops crossed the Potomac River from Virginia and made their way through Maryland and Pennsylvania. They neared the town of Gettysburg, Pennsylvania, in late June. Lee was surprised to learn of Meade's promotion. He was also surprised to discover that the Army of the Potomac was closer than he had believed. The Union army was chasing Lee. It had already crossed the Potomac River and was headed toward Gettysburg.

Before the Civil War, General George Meade had served with distinction in both the Second Seminole War and the Mexican-American War.

General Meade realized that Gettysburg was an excellent location to make a stand against Lee's forces.

The Perfect Battlefield

The first Union forces arrived in Gettysburg on June 30. General John Buford's **cavalry** reached the town well before the main army. Buford was ordered to hold possession of the town until reinforcements could arrive.

The Union forces wanted to hold the town because it made an excellent spot to face off against Lee's army. The surrounding geography offered plenty of easily defensible locations. South of the town were two long ridges: Seminary Ridge and, to the east of it, Cemetery Ridge. Cemetery Ridge led north to two hills, called Cemetery Hill and Culp's Hill. Two other hills were located at the south end of the ridge. They were known as Big Round Top and Little Round Top. Near them were a peach orchard and a wheat field.

A small group of Confederates headed toward Gettysburg to look for supplies on the same day Buford and his men arrived. They immediately went back to warn the rest of the Confederate army.

Cemetery Ridge would prove to be a major strategic point in the Battle of Gettysburg.

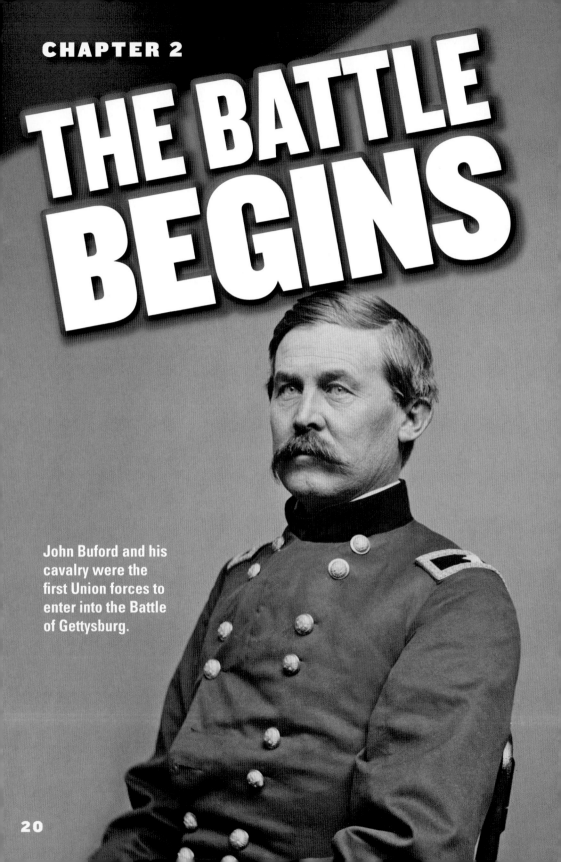

CHAPTER 2

THE BATTLE BEGINS

John Buford and his cavalry were the first Union forces to enter into the Battle of Gettysburg.

ON THE MORNING OF JULY 1, 1863, a group of Confederate forces headed into Gettysburg to gather **reconnaissance**. They encountered Buford's cavalry forces. The first shots of the Battle of Gettysburg were fired at around 8:00 a.m. What began as a small **skirmish** between the reconnaissance forces and the cavalry would soon expand into a three-day battle between the country's most powerful armies.

Tens of thousands of Union and Confederate soldiers clashed at Gettysburg.

Opening Moves

The Confederate forces attacked Gettysburg from the west and north. Buford's forces were greatly outnumbered at this early point in the battle. There were about 28,000 Confederates fighting around 18,000 Union soldiers. **Infantry** from both sides clashed. Buford knew that he could not win the fight. But the Union forces would be in a good position for the rest of the battle if he could hold out until reinforcements arrived.

Union reinforcements commanded by General John Reynolds began arriving at around 10:00 a.m. Reynolds surveyed the situation. He took note of the surrounding landscape and the enemy positions. He then immediately wrote a report for General Meade. Reynolds feared that the Confederate forces would be able to take the high ground before the Union had a chance to control it. He gave his report to a messenger after finishing it. Reynolds was shot in the head and killed almost immediately afterward.

General Lee arrived at the battlefield around this time. He had not wanted to begin the battle with the small-scale combat taking place when he arrived. His original plan was to gather up his forces and open with

General Reynolds (left) was killed soon after sending his report to General Meade.

YESTERDAY'S HEADLINES

The people of Gettysburg reacted in a variety of ways when the battle began. A man named John Burns went into the streets with his own gun to fight alongside Union forces and was wounded several times. President Lincoln visited Burns to thank him during his trip to Gettysburg after the battle.

Some townspeople, such as Sallie Myers, Daniel Skelly, and Tillie Pierce, cared for injured soldiers. An attorney and local leader named David McConaughy ran a group of civilian scouts that spied on Confederate forces in the region in late June 1863. McConaughy passed critical information about Confederate troop movements to Union commanders at the start of the Gettysburg battle.

a strong attack. He had hoped to win the fight quickly and continue moving into the North. But now the fight had already begun. He had no choice but to change his strategy.

Taking the High Ground

General Reynolds's message reached General Meade in Taneytown, Maryland, about 20 miles (32 kilometers) south of Gettysburg. Meade quickly sent Commander Winfield Hancock to Gettysburg. Hancock was given orders to take control of the forces there. Hancock saw Cemetery Ridge and the surrounding hills upon arriving. He said, "I think this is the

General Ewell's wooden leg benefited him in the early stages of the battle, when it, instead of his real leg, was hit by a bullet.

strongest position by nature upon which to fight a battle that I ever saw."

The Union forces began a strategic retreat toward Cemetery Ridge. They planned to join up with General Meade's forces when they arrived there later in the day. Lee also realized the strategic importance of this location. He ordered General Richard Ewell to take it for the Confederacy. But Ewell's forces had suffered heavy casualties in the early part of the battle. About 8,000 men had been killed or wounded. Ewell had been shot as well. But luckily the bullet hit his wooden leg. He had received the wooden leg after losing his real leg in an earlier battle of the war.

Ewell did not follow Lee's orders immediately. He took time to regroup his scattered men before attempting to take Cemetery Ridge. This would prove to be a costly delay. The Union forces were allowed to reach the ridge first. They then began forming into a hook shape along the high ground southeast of Gettysburg. These efforts helped them secure a highly defensible position. The Union was able to regroup. They had suffered about 10,000 casualties that day. General Meade arrived late that night with reinforcements and began planning for the next day's fight.

The Second Day

Union forces gathered along Cemetery Ridge on the morning of July 2. Meanwhile, General Lee consulted with his officers. General James Longstreet encouraged

Ewell's hesitation allowed the Union to hold the high ground at Cemetery Ridge.

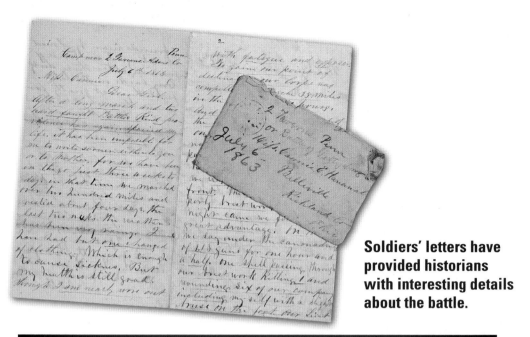

Soldiers' letters have provided historians with interesting details about the battle.

A FIRSTHAND LOOK AT
SOLDIERS' LETTERS

Soldiers often spent months away from their homes and families during the Civil War. Without modern conveniences such as telephones or e-mail, soldiers wrote letters to their families to tell of their experiences and ask what was happening at home. Many soldiers' letters survive today. They offer a look into what life was like for the troops. See page 60 for a link to a site that shows soldiers' actual handwritten letters.

Lee to march the army south to find a more defensible position. Then they could force the Union army to come to them. Longstreet knew that they were allowing the Union to choose where the battle was fought. But Lee disagreed with Longstreet. "They are there in position," he said, "and I am going to whip them or they are going to whip me."

The two sides fought viciously for control of the Round Tops.

Clash at the Round Tops

Little Round Top, at the southern end of Cemetery Ridge, was undefended. Both sides quickly realized its importance. The Confederate forces could fire down on the Union army with cannons if they were allowed to claim the top of the hill. Confederate forces began moving toward the hill. Meade sent a **brigade** to take the hill and keep the Confederates from reaching its top. Colonel Joshua Chamberlain and his troops were part of the brigade.

Chamberlain and 386 Union soldiers reached the top of the hill as Confederate forces began climbing up from its base. The Union soldiers fired down on them.

Many Confederates were killed. The Union forces soon began to run out of **ammunition**. Chamberlain ordered his men to charge the advancing Confederates. The Union soldiers surged down the hill with their **bayonets** pointing forward. Hundreds of Confederates were stabbed to death. The survivors were soon forced to withdraw.

A Fight in the Wheat Field

Lee ordered General Longstreet to make an attack on Cemetery Ridge. Longstreet slowly moved toward the Round Top hills instead. On his way, his forces collided

The fighting at Little Round Top left many men dead or wounded.

Joshua Chamberlain

Joshua Chamberlain is often considered one of the heroes of the Battle of Gettysburg. He was born in 1828 in Maine. Before the war he was a professor at Maine's Bowdoin College. When the war began, he asked permission to leave his position at the college to join the army. The college denied his request. He left anyway.

Chamberlain left the military in 1866. He then returned to Bowdoin College to become president of the school. He also served as governor of Maine and later ran a railroad construction company.

with General Daniel Sickles's troops in the wheat field. Meade had ordered Sickles to take Little Round Top earlier in the day. Sickles chose to move his forces toward the peach orchard and wheat field located near the hill instead. This turned out to be an excellent decision.

Both sides took losses in the wheat field. General Sickles lost a leg, but the Union forces eventually drove back Longstreet's men. In choosing to occupy the wheat field, Sickles kept the Confederate forces from advancing on Cemetery Ridge from the south.

The End of the Day

There were several other scenes of combat on the second day. Lee sent Ewell to attack Culp's Hill at the north end of Cemetery Ridge. Lee also sent General A. P. Hill to attack the main Union force at the center of the ridge.

The Union suffered heavy losses. But it was able to hold on to its position along the ridge.

General Meade met with his officers that night. Meade feared that the Union forces were not strong enough to hold the high ground for another day after experiencing such heavy losses. Meade asked his officers if they should stay and fight, or retreat to a location where they could resupply. If they stayed, he asked, should they attack first, or wait for Lee to make the first move? He also asked how long they should wait for Lee to attack.

The officers agreed that they should stay on the ridge and await Lee's attack. Meade predicted that Lee would attack the center of the ridge the next day because he had already failed in his attempt to take the hills to the north and south. Meade and his officers began planning the best ways to fight off an attack on their center.

Meade believed that Lee would make an attack on the Union's center.

CHAPTER 3

A BLOODY CONCLUSION

General Longstreet believed that continuing the fight at Gettysburg was a poor strategy.

BOTH SIDES WERE BRUISED AND bloodied after two days of combat. The Confederate forces began preparing for a third day of fighting. Longstreet once again urged Lee to withdraw and move south to wait for a Union attack. Lee once again dismissed his general's idea.

Lee believed that the Confederates were sure to lose the battle if it went on too long.

Planning the Final Attack

The Confederates lacked a supply line because they were in enemy territory. They restocked by taking what they needed as they passed through towns. Thus, Lee believed they needed to keep the army moving. Waiting in one place for the Union to attack first would result in running out of supplies. Lee needed to win in Gettysburg and get back on the move northward.

Lee turned to his original battle plan by focusing his army's strength in one massive attack. The attack would begin with a huge **artillery** assault on Cemetery Ridge. This would be followed by a charge at the center of the Union forces. Smaller forces would circle around to the north and rear of the ridge.

At dawn on July 3, Union artillery began firing on General Ewell's forces near Culp's Hill. Lee and Longstreet prepared for the main charge. Lee decided that General George Pickett's **division** would lead the attack. Pickett and his men were a part of Longstreet's **corps**. Longstreet began arranging the 15,000 soldiers. He placed about 160 artillery units along each side of the force.

Following Lee's orders, Longstreet chose Pickett to head the charge against the Union.

Pickett's Charge

Longstreet signaled for the artillery to begin firing on Cemetery Ridge shortly after 1:00 p.m. The two sides exchanged heavy artillery fire for the next two hours. Smoke covered the battlefield. But little damage was done to either side. Pickett asked Longstreet's permission to begin the attack as the cannon fire began to slow down. Longstreet still believed that the plan was a bad idea. But he was under direct orders from Lee. He nodded to Pickett. The Confederate forces began surging forward.

The Confederates had to cross about 1 mile (1.6 km) of open field to reach Cemetery Ridge. They became easy targets for the Union soldiers. The Confederates fell out of formation as men began to fall. The Union soldiers carefully organized waves of concentrated

Pickett's Charge turned out to be a major disaster for the Confederates.

gunfire, cutting down large numbers of Confederate soldiers at once. More than half of the 12,500 Confederate troops who participated in the charge were killed. Only a few hundred made it all the way into the center of the Union forces.

The smaller forces that Lee sent to attack the Union forces from the north and the rear fared no better. One force was stopped early in the morning. Union troops intercepted the other force when it was still 3 miles (4.8 km) from reaching its attack position.

Only one hour after Pickett's men began their charge, the Battle of Gettysburg was over. Confederate forces were forced to retreat. The Union was victorious.

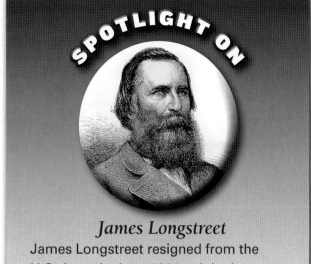

SPOTLIGHT ON

James Longstreet

James Longstreet resigned from the U.S. Army in June 1861 to join the Confederacy. He was not an enthusiastic supporter of secession. But he was a strong believer in states' rights. Some historians blame Longstreet for the Confederate loss at Gettysburg. They believe that he was too slow to organize Pickett's Charge because of the disagreement with Lee. Others place the blame on Lee's overconfidence in believing that his army could successfully attack such a strong position.

Longstreet joined the antislavery Republican Party after the war and became active in the U.S. government. Some Southerners, who believed he was a traitor to Confederate beliefs, hated Longstreet.

Thousands of soldiers were left dead on the battlefield.

The Aftermath

Thousands of dying and injured soldiers were strewn across the Gettysburg battlefield. Smoke filled the air. Blood covered the ground. More than 3,200 Union troops and 4,500 Confederates had been killed. Over 20,000 men on each side were injured or missing. Five thousand horses and mules had also been killed in the fighting.

A GETTYSBURG BATTLEFIELD MAP

In the years immediately following the war, countless books, photos, diaries, letters, and other materials relating to the war were published. Worldwide interest in the American Civil War is extremely strong even today. Battlefield maps are of particular interest to students of the conflict. See page 60 for a link to view a map showing troop positions at Gettysburg on the second day of battle. The map was probably drawn in 1864 or 1865. It even includes the names of several Gettysburg townspeople.

General Lee congratulated the surviving soldiers for their bravery as they returned to him. "It has been a sad, sad day to us," Lee said. "I never saw troops behave more magnificently than Pickett's division of Virginians did today." Lee knew that the results of the battle were in many ways his fault. Making such a charge on the Union forces had been a mistake. So had allowing the Union to choose where the battle would be fought. Longstreet's advice had proven to be sound. "You men have done all that men can do," he told his troops. "The fault is certainly my own."

The Retreat

Lee began moving the Army of Northern Virginia back to the South on July 4, 1863. The Confederacy would never again fight in Union territory. Lee was so ashamed of his loss that he offered his resignation to Confederate president Jefferson Davis. Davis refused the offer. But Lee saw Gettysburg as a personal failure.

The Confederates encountered a delay at the Potomac River as they marched back toward Virginia. Confederate troops had built a bridge to cross the river on their way north. Union forces later burned it. Now, Lee and his men had no way to cross back into the South. The Confederates were forced to wait at the river. They expected Union forces to soon close in on them. Lee indicated in letters to his wife and President Davis that he feared his army would meet its end on the banks of the Potomac.

Lee and his soldiers fled Gettysburg through heavy rain.

Meade set up headquarters at Gettysburg, hoping that his men could rest.

Meade's Mistake

Lee did not need to fear Meade's army. The Union commander did not think it was necessary to attack the Confederate forces as they retreated. He believed that simply driving the Confederates from Union soil was a sufficient victory. Meade also wanted to rest his troops. He claimed that they were "worn out by long marches and three days' hard fighting."

The Army of the Potomac went on to fight in several other major battles during the Civil War.

President Lincoln was furious that Meade did not pursue Lee and crush the Confederates. Lincoln believed that Lee's total defeat would be a major step toward ending the war. He was also frustrated by Meade's belief that keeping Confederates out of Union territory was the primary goal of the conflict. "Will our Generals never get that idea out of their heads?" Lincoln asked. "The whole country is our soil." Meade offered his resignation to the president. Lincoln refused and forgave him for his lack of aggression. Meade commanded the Army of the Potomac for the rest of the war.

The Turning Point

Many people believe the war could have been ended sooner if Meade had pressed his attack against Lee. But the Battle of Gettysburg was still a major victory for the Union. The entire war was fought on Southern soil after Gettysburg. This soon took its toll on the Confederates' supplies and resources. They were constantly on the defensive. Attacks from the Union eventually shut down their railroads and caused them to run out of necessary supplies. By the end of the war in 1865, some Confederate soldiers were even forced to go barefoot and fight without ammunition.

Later in the war, many Confederate soldiers went without basic needs such as clothing and bullets.

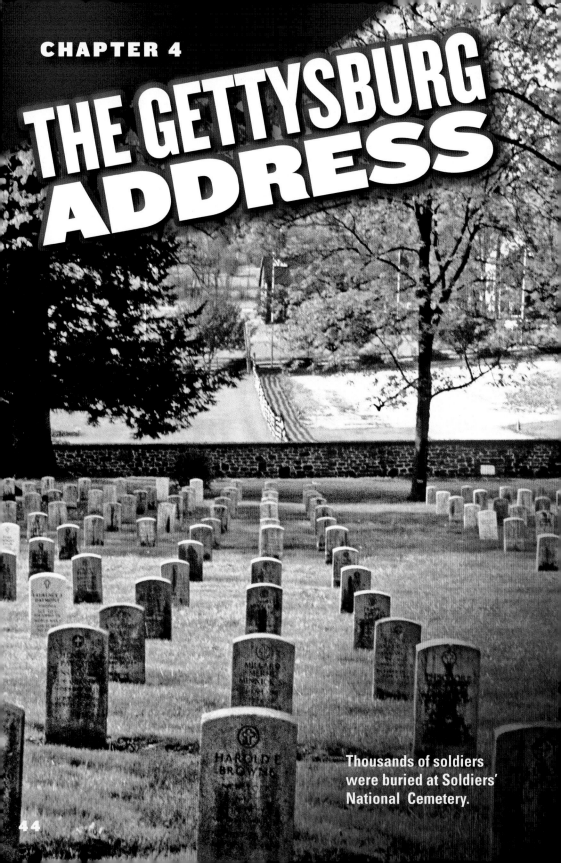

CHAPTER 4

THE GETTYSBURG ADDRESS

Thousands of soldiers were buried at Soldiers' National Cemetery.

THOUSANDS OF DEAD BODIES

lay on the Gettysburg battlefield when the fighting stopped. Bodies of both Union and Confederate soldiers were buried in shallow graves on the battlefield or along roads. The Union dead were buried quickly. But many Confederate bodies were left unburied for days.

Pennsylvania Governor Andrew Curtain decided that something needed to be done about the bodies. He hired Gettysburg resident David Wills to create a cemetery honoring the dead soldiers. Soldiers' National Cemetery included over 3,000 graves when Wills finished it in November 1863. More than 1,200 of them were for unidentified bodies.

Edward Everett had served as a U.S. representative, a U.S. senator, and the governor of Massachusetts.

Honoring the Dead

Wills decided that an event should be held to mark the cemetery's opening. He sent out two invitations to well-known public figures, asking them to speak at the event. The first invitation went to a former politician and popular speaker named Edward Everett. The other went to President Abraham Lincoln. Both accepted.

Lincoln believed that the opening of the cemetery would be an excellent occasion to share his ideas about the state of the country. He began writing his speech weeks before the dedication. He worked through several drafts to include the right words to express his thoughts about those who had died at Gettysburg. Lincoln wanted to reinforce his idea that the country should come together once again. He also wanted to honor the men who died at Gettysburg and inspire the surviving Union troops to continue their fight.

President Lincoln arrived in Gettysburg on November 18, 1863. He continued to make changes to his speech even on the night before he was to deliver it.

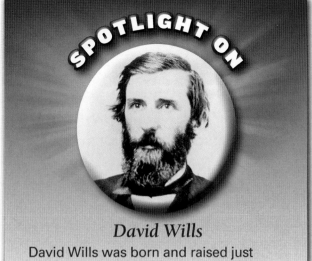

SPOTLIGHT ON

David Wills

David Wills was born and raised just a few miles outside of Gettysburg. He lived in the area his entire life, attending Gettysburg College and becoming a lawyer and school administrator. He witnessed the Battle of Gettysburg firsthand as soldiers fought in the streets outside his door. Wills and his neighbors hid from the fighting in his cellar.

Wills visited the Gettysburg battlefield with Governor Curtain just a few days after the fighting ended. They immediately realized how important a cemetery would be. Wills invited the president to the opening of the cemetery, although he did not think Lincoln would attend.

Dedication of a Cemetery

On November 19, 1863, about 15,000 people gathered in the cool fall weather to mark the opening of the new cemetery. The crowd was filled with government officials and reporters. It also contained many soldiers and local townspeople.

Lincoln arrived on horseback. He wore his customary stovepipe hat. He wore a band of mourning around the hat. He mourned not just for the soldiers, but also for his young son who had died the previous year.

The event began with music and prayers. Then Everett spoke. He talked for more than two hours. Some of his

People came from all around for a chance to hear President Lincoln speak at the dedication of the cemetery in Gettysburg.

Each of Lincoln's drafts of the speech is slightly different from the others.

words spoke against the Confederacy. "I speak of it as a crime," he said of the secession, "because the Constitution of the United States so regards it, and puts 'rebellion' on par with 'invasion.'" President Lincoln was announced as the next speaker once Everett had concluded.

A FIRSTHAND LOOK AT
PRESIDENT LINCOLN'S SPEECH

President Lincoln made five drafts of his speech at Gettysburg, known as the Gettysburg Address. He borrowed language from the Declaration of Independence when he said, "all men are created equal." The earliest known draft of the address is called the Nicolay Copy. This is because it was once owned by John George Nicolay, Lincoln's private secretary. See page 60 for a link to view the document, in Lincoln's handwriting.

The audience listened carefully to President Lincoln's words.

Lincoln's Words

Lincoln did not take sides during his speech. He spoke not of the Union or the Confederacy, but simply of the men who died. He honored their sacrifice. It did not matter which side they had fought on. His words conveyed his strong belief that the Union and the Confederacy were not separate nations in conflict. They were two parts of a greater whole.

He also spoke of a desire to ensure that the men who died on the battlefield at Gettysburg had not done so in vain. He presented the war as "unfinished work" and asked that the people of the United States take the soldiers' deaths as inspiration to work even harder toward unifying the country. His speech lasted about three minutes.

After the Speech

President Lincoln had managed to give one of the most memorable and powerful speeches in U.S. history. But Lincoln himself did not think the speech went well. He called it "a flat failure."

"The world will little note, nor long remember what we say here," Lincoln said during the speech. But the Gettysburg Address is today considered one of the greatest examples of what one can accomplish with just a few words. In mere moments, Lincoln transformed the way people viewed the war.

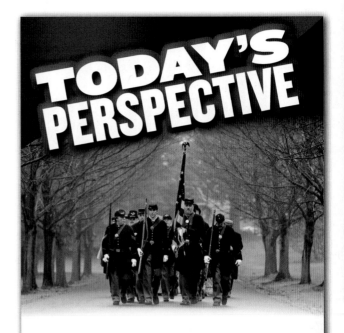

TODAY'S PERSPECTIVE

The year 2011 marked the 150th anniversary of the beginning of the Civil War. Museums, historical societies, and other organizations around the United States arranged events to commemorate the historic occasion. Fort Sumter National Monument held reenactments of the famous battle that signaled the war's start. People gathered in Gettysburg in 2010 to celebrate the 147th anniversary of the Gettysburg Address.

Some people from southern states even celebrated the secession. In Montgomery, Alabama, people held a parade and reenacted the swearing in of Confederate president Jefferson Davis.

What Happened Where?

July 1

Gener Lee

SEMINARY RIDGE

Ju

"Picket Charge

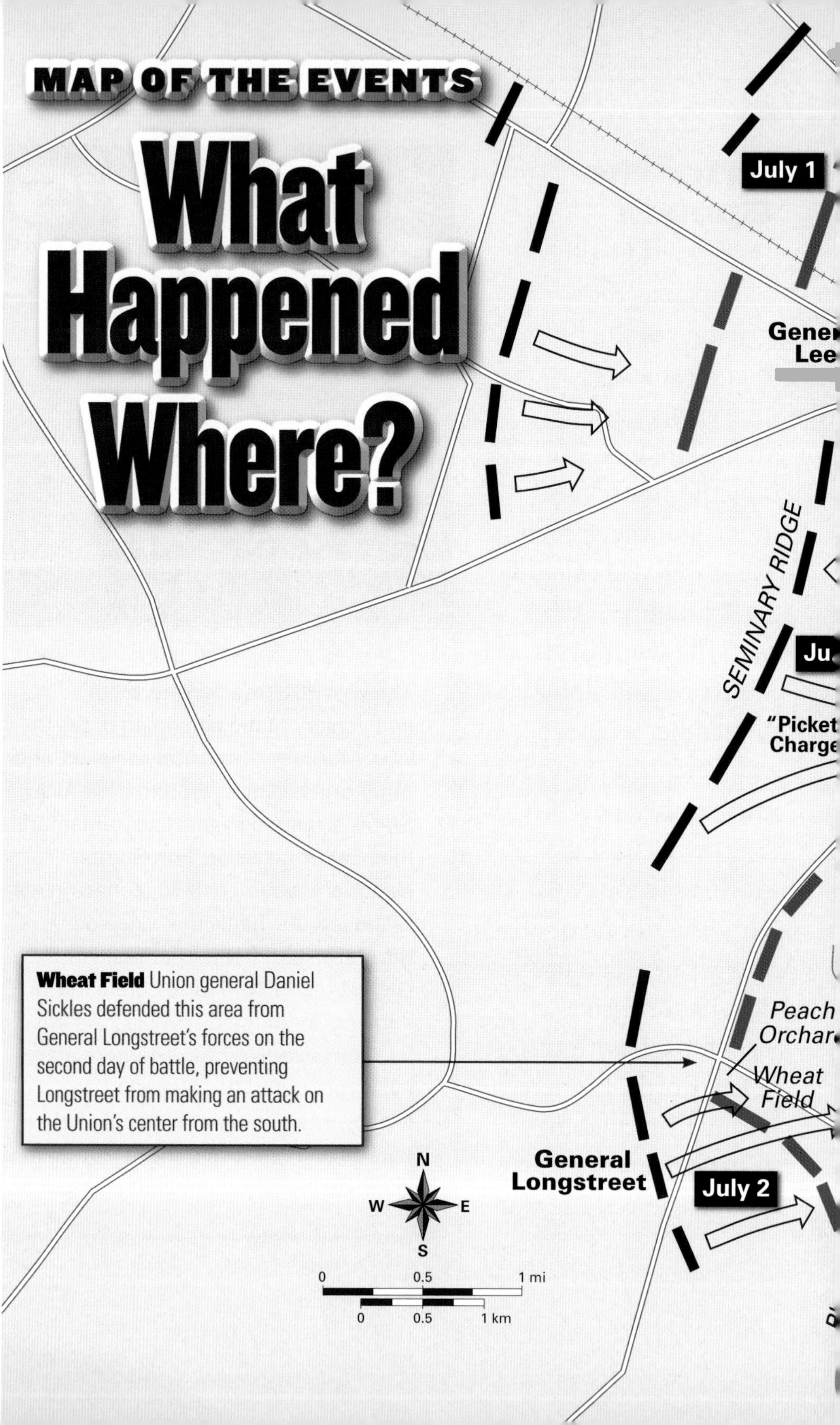

Wheat Field Union general Daniel Sickles defended this area from General Longstreet's forces on the second day of battle, preventing Longstreet from making an attack on the Union's center from the south.

Peach Orchar

Wheat Field

General Longstreet

July 2

N
W   E
S

| 0 | 0.5 | 1 mi |
| 0 | 0.5 | 1 km |

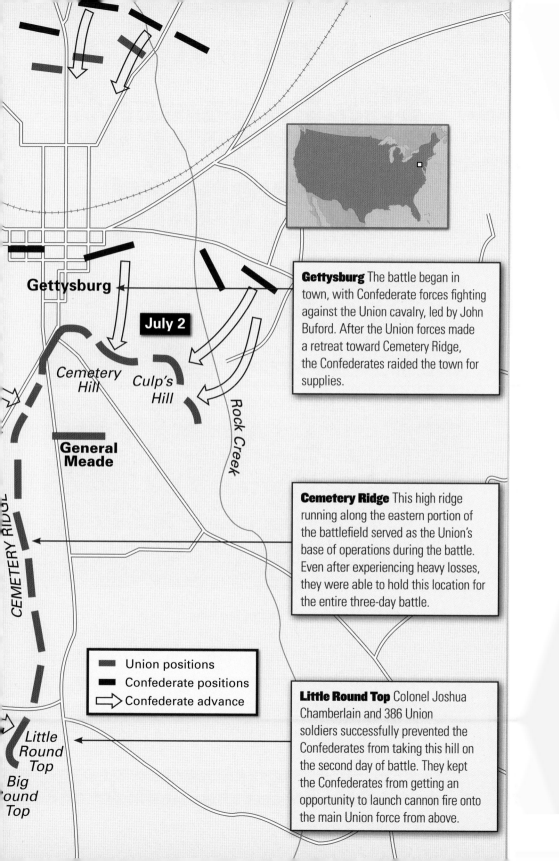

Gettysburg

July 2

Cemetery Hill

Culp's Hill

General Meade

Rock Creek

CEMETERY RIDGE

Gettysburg The battle began in town, with Confederate forces fighting against the Union cavalry, led by John Buford. After the Union forces made a retreat toward Cemetery Ridge, the Confederates raided the town for supplies.

Cemetery Ridge This high ridge running along the eastern portion of the battlefield served as the Union's base of operations during the battle. Even after experiencing heavy losses, they were able to hold this location for the entire three-day battle.

Union positions

Confederate positions

Confederate advance

Little Round Top Colonel Joshua Chamberlain and 386 Union soldiers successfully prevented the Confederates from taking this hill on the second day of battle. They kept the Confederates from getting an opportunity to launch cannon fire onto the main Union force from above.

Little Round Top

Big Round Top

The Legacy of Gettysburg

Lee's surrender marked the end of the war.

The Civil War ended in spring 1865. On April 9, General Lee surrendered to Union general Ulysses S. Grant at Appomattox Court House in Virginia. President Lincoln was shot and killed just five days after Lee's surrender.

JOHN WILKES BOOTH WAS

His killer was John Wilkes Booth, a supporter of the Confederacy and a strong believer in slavery.

Congress enacted the 13th Amendment to the U.S. Constitution on December 6, 1865. This amendment officially made slavery illegal in the United States. It was a major step forward. But African Americans continued to struggle against poor treatment and discrimination for many decades. Racial division in the United States is a major problem even today.

The American Civil War was originally fought to preserve the Union. It took on greater meaning during the years of fighting. Lincoln eventually made the importance of victory not only about preservation but also liberation, most notably that of America's slaves. A Union defeat, or a compromise with slaveholding Southern states, would have made liberation and freedom impossible.

Only victory could accomplish Lincoln's worthy goal. But he needed successes on the battlefield to do it. The Union victory at the Battle of Gettysburg was one of the most significant events that helped bring the war to its end and put the nation on the road to reuniting and healing.

Edward Everett (1794–1865) was a politician and lecturer who spoke before President Lincoln did at the Gettysburg cemetery dedication ceremony.

Robert E. Lee (1807–1870) was the commander of the Army of Northern Virginia at the Battle of Gettysburg.

Jefferson Davis (1808–1889) was the president of the Confederate States of America.

Abraham Lincoln (1809–1865) was the U.S. president during the Civil War.

George G. Meade (1815–1872) was the commander of the Army of the Potomac at the Battle of Gettysburg.

Richard Ewell (1817–1872) was the Confederate officer who failed to take Cemetery Ridge on the first day of the battle.

Richard Ewell

Daniel Sickles (1819–1914) was the Union general whose decision to occupy the wheat field instead of the Round Top hills prevented a major Confederate attack.

James Longstreet (1821–1904) was the Confederate general who advised Robert E. Lee to retreat and find a better position from which to fight.

George Pickett (1825–1875) was the Confederate general whose men made the fateful attack that caused the Confederate forces to lose the Battle of Gettysburg.

John Buford (1826–1863) was the Union cavalry officer who was first to arrive in Gettysburg.

Joshua Chamberlain (1828–1914) was the Union officer whose troops defended Little Round Top during the second day of battle.

Joshua Chamberlain

David Wills (1831–1894) designed Soldiers' National Cemetery at Gettysburg.

TIMELINE

1860

November 6
Abraham Lincoln is elected president.

December 20
South Carolina becomes the first state to secede from the Union.

1861

April 12
The American Civil War begins when Confederate soldiers fire on Fort Sumter.

1863

1865

June
General Lee begins moving north from Virginia into Union territory.

July 1
The Battle of Gettysburg begins as Confederate reconnaissance forces clash with Union general John Buford's cavalry.

July 2
The Union forces take heavy casualties but hold on to high ground outside Gettysburg.

July 3
The Confederate forces are defeated after the failure of Pickett's Charge.

November 19
President Lincoln gives the Gettysburg Address.

April 9
The Civil War ends.

LIVING HISTORY

Primary sources provide firsthand evidence about a topic. Witnesses to a historical event create primary sources. They include autobiographies, newspaper reports of the time, oral histories, photographs, and memoirs. A secondary source analyzes primary sources, and is one step or more removed from the event. Secondary sources include textbooks, encyclopedias, and commentaries.

Draft of President Lincoln's Gettysburg Address Five original, handwritten copies of the Gettysburg Address are known to exist. To view the earliest draft, known as the Nicolay Copy, go to *www.loc.gov/exhibits/treasures/trt034.html*

Fort Sumter Political Cartoon A political cartoon of the time showed South Carolina's governor threatening President James Buchanan to surrender Fort Sumter to the South. To view the original cartoon, go to *http://loc.gov/pictures/resource/cph.3a19458/*

Gettysburg Battlefield Map To view a hand-drawn map of the positions of Union and Confederate forces on July 2, 1863, the second day of fighting at Gettysburg, go to *http://memory.loc.gov/cgi-bin/query/h?ammem/gmd:@field%28NUMBER+@band%28g3824g+cwh00160%29%29*

Soldiers' Letters To view original letters written by Civil War soldiers go to *http://content.lib.washington.edu/cdm4/browse.php?CISOROOT=/civilwar*

RESOURCES

Books

Butzer, C. M. *Gettysburg: The Graphic Novel*. New York: HarperCollins, 2009.

Fradin, Dennis B. *The Battle of Gettysburg*. New York: Marshall Cavendish Benchmark, 2008.

Kennedy, Robert F., Jr. *Joshua Chamberlain and the American Civil War*. New York: Hyperion Books for Children, 2007.

Phillips, Ellen Blue. *Abraham Lincoln: From Pioneer to President*. New York: Sterling, 2007.

Rappaport, Doreen. *Abe's Honest Words: The Life of Abraham Lincoln*. New York: Hyperion Books for Children, 2008.

Salmon, John S. *Historic Photos of Gettysburg*. Nashville: Turner, 2007.

Weber, Jennifer L. *Summer's Bloodiest Days: The Battle of Gettysburg As Told from All Sides*. Washington, DC: National Geographic, 2010.

Web Sites

Library of Congress—Gettysburg Address
http://myloc.gov/exhibitions/gettysburgaddress/Pages/default.aspx
Find out how the Library of Congress preserves Lincoln's original handwritten copies of the Gettysburg Address.

Library of Congress—Selected Civil War Photographs
http://memory.loc.gov/ammem/cwphtml/cwphome.html
Check out some interesting photographs taken during the Civil War.

PBS—The Civil War: Fact Sheet
www.pbs.org/civilwar/war/facts.html
Read a fascinating fact sheet with little-known details about the Civil War.

GLOSSARY

ammunition (am-yuh-NISH-uhn) things such as bullets or cannonballs that can be fired from weapons

artillery (ar-TIL-uh-ree) large, powerful guns that are mounted on wheels or tracks

bayonets (BAY-uh-nets) long blades that are attached to the ends of rifles

brigade (bri-GAYD) a unit of soldiers numbering 3,000 to 5,000

cavalry (KAV-uhl-ree) soldiers mounted on horseback

civil war (SIV-uhl WAR) a war fought between residents of the same country

compromise (KOM-pruh-mize) an agreement between two sides that requires each to give up something that it wants

corps (KOR) a unit of soldiers numbering 20,000 to 45,000

division (di-VIZH-uhn) a unit of soldiers numbering 10,000 to 15,000

enlisted (en-LIST-id) joined the armed forces

infantry (IN-fuhn-tree) soldiers who fight on foot

neutral (NOO-truhl) not supporting any side of a conflict

reconnaissance (ruh-KAHN-uh-sihns) information gathered from a search of the area

skirmish (SKIR-mish) a minor fight in war

INDEX

Page numbers in *italics* indicate illustrations.

ABOUT THE AUTHOR

Josh Gregory received a BA in English at the University of Missouri-Columbia. He lives in Chicago, Illinois.